D-DAY

By Brad Silliman

INSIDE FRONT COVER:

Map shows three European war fronts as year 1944 began. Germans were on the defensive on the Russian front and in Italy and were expecting an Allied invasion in a stretch of western Europe running from Norway to southern France.

Germans prepared a 1,200-mile stretch of coast of France, Belgium and the Netherlands for an expected Allied invasion in 1944. Here a single Nazi soldier mans a machine gun on the German-held coast overlooking the English Channel.

© Copyright 1979. International Media Systems, Inc.
P.O. Box 178, Longwood, Florida 32750
All Rights Reserved
Printed in U.S.A.

All photographs in this book are property of Wide World Photos, Inc., New York, N.Y. 10020.

TABLE OF CONTENTS

Chapter 1
Blitzkreig!... 5

Chapter 2
Fortress Europe.................................. 10

Chapter 3
Death Zone....................................... 18

Chapter 4
Bolero... 24

Chapter 5
Fortitude... 32

Chapter 6
Pointblank.. 36

Chapter 7
Neptune.. 42

Chapter 8
Okay. We'll go!................................. 51

Chapter 9
Airborne... 57

Chapter 10
Confusion... 66

Chapter 11
H-Hour... 69

Chapter 12
Bloody Omaha.................................. 78

Chapter 13
Sword, Juno, Gold............................ 88

Chapter 14
On to Berlin!..................................... 91

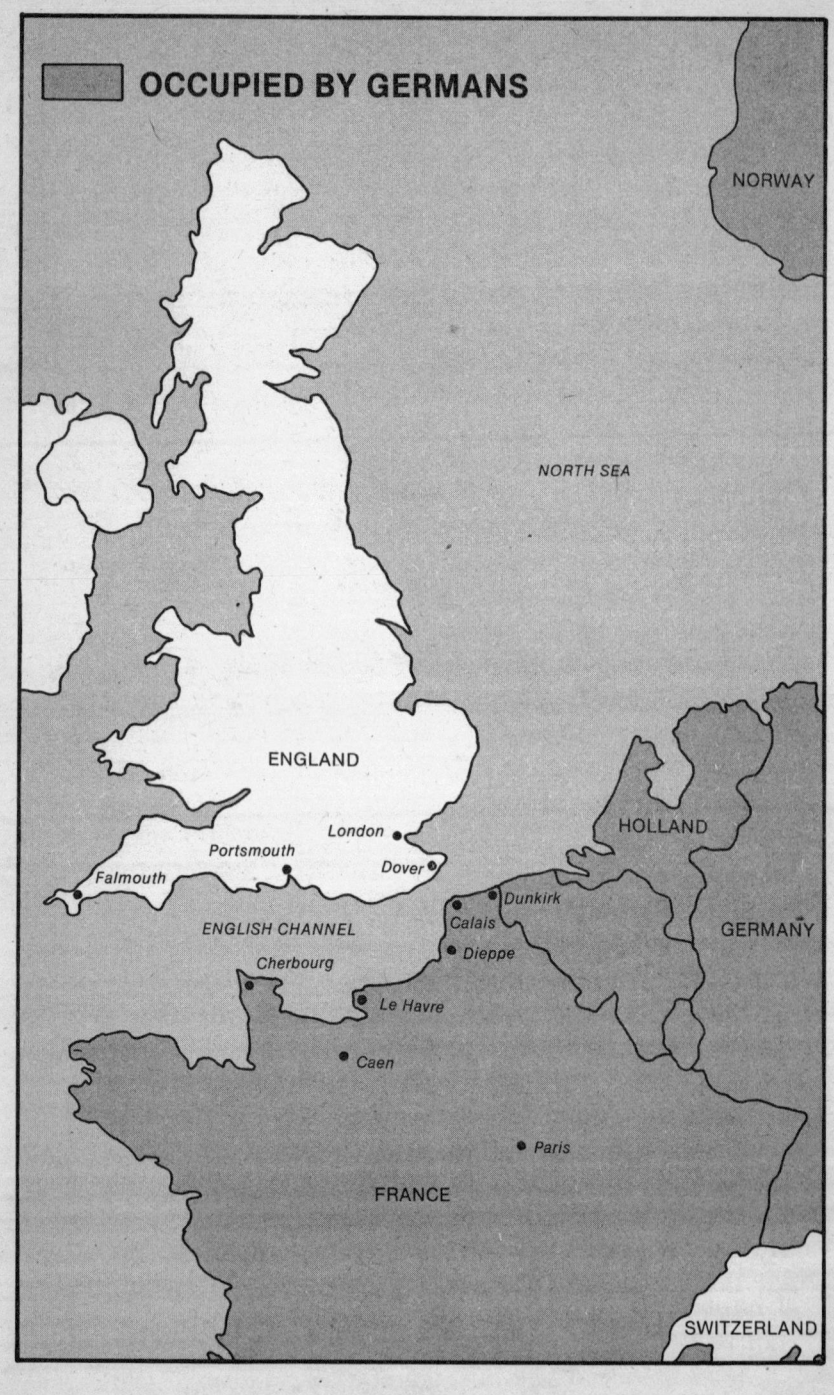

CHAPTER I: *Blitzkrieg!*

On September 1, 1939, without a declaration of war, Nazi Germany invaded Poland. After 18 days of battle Poland was captured except for scattered groups of Polish guerrilla fighters. The swift and brutal slaughter of Poland's small and old-fashioned army was the beginning of World War II.

Using tanks, dive bombers, motorized artillery, armored trucks, motorcycles and paratroops, Germany showed the rest of the world a glimpse of what would happen to most of Europe in a few short years. Germany's dictator, Adolf Hitler, not only planned to rule all of Europe but eventually the entire earth.

Hitler's Nazis took over Germany in 1933. With an almost hypnotic power over the German people, Hitler preached about the superiority of the "master race" and turned the country's energy toward preparing for war.

Germany's industrial leaders were called upon to create a new war technology that would produce the most advanced weapons of that time.

A year before the Polish invasion, Hitler's troops occupied Austria and Czechoslovakia and forced these two countries to become part of Germany. Anyone in either of these countries who disagreed would find himself in a Nazi prison or worse.

Following the conquest of Poland, Germany's

well-trained army marched north and took over Denmark in one day and Norway in six weeks of fighting.

By now, a new phrase had entered the world's vocabulary—Blitzkreig! Meaning "lightning war" in German, this was Hitler's term for modern mobile warfare. This involved tactics using large numbers of panzer divisions (tank units), self-propelled cannons and masses of shock troops in fast-moving half-tracks.

The Wehrmacht (German Army) used commandos who would parachute or land by glider on key bridges or crossroads just before an attack. They were backed up by the sleekest and mightiest air force in Europe.

Because the rest of Europe's armies had not changed their military thinking since the end of World War I, Hitler's crack troops were able to overrun and capture many nations—hardly firing a shot. Some countries gave up without a fight because their leaders felt it was a suicidal waste of lives to oppose such armed might.

In late Spring of 1940, Germany shocked the world by capturing Holland, Belgium, Luxembourg and France in 56 days. The battered survivors of this blitzkrieg, 300,000 British and French troops, were driven into the sea at Dunkirk where many were rescued off the beach by British ships and boats which came across the English Channel.

For a time, the Germans planned an immediate invasion of England but Hitler decided he would have plenty of time later and turned his attention elsewhere.

Nazi troops next marched into Yugoslavia and Greece to add these countries to Hitler's growing list of conquests. At the same time, Communist Russia, with whom Hitler had signed a peace treaty, was busily gobbling up all territories in eastern Europe the Nazis did not occupy.

For most Europeans living under Nazi rule, life

was miserable at best. The Nazis drained them of raw materials, food supplies, precious metals, money, art and people. The people were used as slave laborers in German factories.

Hitler's "new world order" called for the liquidation (murder) or enslavement of Jews, Slavs, Russians, Poles, Czechoslovaks and Gypsies. Jews were especially targeted for death by Hitler. The Nazis used them as a scapegoat for all of Germany's past problems.

In Poland, as soon as the Nazis took over, concentration and extermination camps were set up to deal with Jews and Polish citizens considered dangerous to German plans. Five million Poles would die in these camps before the end of the war, three million of them Jewish.

Breaking his treaty with the Russians, Hitler's troops invaded the Soviet Union in June 1941. His goal was to destroy the Russian Army and the Communist Party and to enslave the largest country in the world.

At the same time, Hitler's allies, Japan and Italy, were seizing new territories of their own. Italy planned to conquer Africa. Japan aimed at kicking all Western powers out of the Pacific, dominating China and ruling half the globe. These three small but ambitious countries were formed into an alliance called the Axis.

For a time, Great Britain and Russia fought almost alone against the Axis. Men fought and died in the air over the English Channel, on the high seas, and in the deserts and dusty towns of North Africa where Britain controlled much of the wealth and where Europe got most of its oil.

In December 1941, without warning, Japan began attacking American military bases in the Pacific and invading territories controlled by the U.S. This brought America into the war.

The British, Americans and Russians formed a

league of countries opposed to the Axis and became known as the Allies. Also included in the Allied nations were Canada, Australia, New Zealand and other countries of the British Empire. Fighting alongside Allied troops would be soldiers who had escaped from the Nazi occupied countries of Europe.

Over the next two years, the armies of the Axis were slowed and finally halted in their mad grab for the world. The Italians, under Dictator Benito Mussolini, had been beaten badly in Africa by the British and Hitler had sent an army to help them.

After two years of bloody battles under the desert sun, the Germans and Italians were doing poorly in Africa. British and American troops had them on the run. Allied air power made all the difference. American and British bombers disrupted the Axis supply lines time and again, and German and Italian tanks would often have to be abandoned on the desert for lack of gasoline.

In Russia, the swift conquest by the Germans had finally been stalled by determined Russian soldiers. And by the end of 1943 the situation had shifted in favor of the Soviet Union.

In the fall of 1943, Allied troops invaded Southern Italy. This caused the immediate downfall of Mussolini's government. German troops moved quickly into Italy and at the end of 1943 held the central and northern portions of that country.

At the beginning of 1944, the German Army was spread out over three battle fronts—the Russian, the Italian and the Atlantic Wall.

Though the Germans were fighting desperately to hold ground in Russia and Italy, the Atlantic Wall was quiet by comparison. The Atlantic Wall, or Western Front, ran from southern France to the tip of Norway. So far, the Allies had not made a serious attempt to invade Western Europe.

However, Germany's military leaders knew it was only a matter of time before an invasion was attempted from England into occupied France.

Hitler knew that if his troops could stop the invasion it would be a while before the Allies made another attempt. This would enable the Germans to send more troops into Russia and Italy and possibly turn the tide of battle on those fronts.

If an Allied invasion succeeded, it meant there would be a third fighting front for the Germans to defend. If this happend, it would only be a matter of time before Nazi Germany was crushed.

When the Allied invasion was finally launched, its commander, American General Dwight D. Eisenhower, would call it a "crusade." For the 300 million Europeans living under Hitler's brutal Nazi regime, it meant the difference between life and death.

CHAPTER II: *Fortress Europe*

By early 1944 the Nazis were certain an Allied invasion was planned for the northwest coast of Europe that year. The big questions were: where and when?

Since August 1942, the Germans had been fortifying the Atlantic coast of Europe from Norway in the north all the way to the French-Spanish border in the south. This was called the Atlantic Wall.

Hitler bragged in radio speeches that these defenses were impregnable and that the Allies would be slaughtered on the beaches. He called the whole of the northwest continent his "Fortress Europe."

These seaside fortifications included bombproof gun emplacements, machine gun positions, underground living and storage areas—all protected by mine fields and barbed wire.

The thickness and strength of these defenses varied according to how suitable a coastal area might be for an enemy invasion site, or beachhead.

For example, many stretches of European coast were sheer cliffs rising from the sea. It was unlikely an invader would attempt to land in these spots. His troops could be picked off by a few riflemen as they attempted to scale the cliffs.

Other coastal areas were protected by underwater

reefs or rock formations which prevented all but the smallest boats from coming ashore.

And other places, such as Holland, were made up of low-lying farmlands close to the sea that could be flooded, preventing the movement of troops and vehicles.

Since the invasion would come from England, the German high command reasoned that Norway and Denmark were too far away to be likely targets. Ships having to deliver the invasion force and keep it supplied would be exposed for a long period to submarine and bomber attack.

German military planners were able to conclude that the invasion would be somewhere in France. They were able to concentrate troops and defenses in areas considered ideal for enemy landings. These would be places with wide, clear beaches where landing craft and ships could unload troops, tanks and supplies. The Allies, the Germans reasoned, would also be looking for sites that were connected by good roads so the invasion troops and vehicles could move inland. The Allies would also need large open fields where paratroops and troop-carrying gliders could land to attack the beach defenses from the rear.

The generals also believed the invasion site would be at or near a deepwater port. If the first stages of an Allied invasion were successful, the British and Americans would soon need a seaport in order to unload their heavier guns and equipment from large ocean-going ships that could not unload at the beaches.

German Field Marshal Gerd von Rundstedt was commander of all German forces in the west. These included 16 divisions in Denmark and Norway, three divisions in Luxembourg, Holland and Belgium and 50 divisions in France. The number of troops available to repulse an enemy invasion in France totaled about 1,300,000.

Rundstedt believed, along with most German military experts, that the invasion would be somewhere between the coastal cities of Dieppe and Calais on either side of the Somme River. He felt an invasion would also be launched against the Normandy area to the south but that this attack would be small and diversionary—designed to draw attention away from the main assault.

The Dieppe-Calais area was the closest part of the French coast to Britain. Calais was only about 20 miles across the Channel from England. It made sense, reasoned the Germans, that the Allies would cross at the shortest water route possible. Their ships could unload and return at a faster rate and their air forces could provide better protection because they could stay in the air longer.

Another reason the Germans believed the Dieppe-Calais coast would be picked by the Allies was because of secret German weapons based there. Hitler had boasted of these weapons and promised that they would turn the tide of war.

British agents had learned in 1943 what these secret weapons were—the V-1 flying bomb and the V-2 rocket. These missiles would soon be launched against London from sites just behind the Calais area. At the same time, in the same area, the Germans were constructing a field gun with 400-foot-long barrels, also aimed at London.

All these weapons, once operating, would be able to deliver one-ton warheads of high explosive into the heart of London around the clock. The Germans thought the Allies would land near the weapons site in order to destroy them as soon as possible.

A third reason Rundstedt felt the Allies would invade the Dieppe-Calais coast was its closeness to the German border.

To a military genius like Rundstedt this was what he would do if he were in the Allies' shoes. As a result, he planned his defense around this theory.

To strengthen his western defenses, Hitler appointed Field Marshal General Erwin Rommel as commander of the Atlantic Wall in November 1943. Rundstedt would still have overall command of the west, but Rommel would have tactical command of troops manning the coastal defenses and most of the troops in France. This collection of units was called Army Group B. It totaled more than one million men.

Rommel, 51 years old, was a young and daring military figure who had led German and Italian forces in Africa. Though the Axis ultimately lost in Africa, it was more because of Allied air strength rather than to the fault of Rommel. The "Desert Fox," as he was nicknamed, was feared and respected by American and British generals. He was popular with the German people and was Hitler's favorite general.

Rommel agreed with Rundstedt that the Dieppe-Calais area was the most likely spot for an Allied beachhead but he disagreed with Rundstedt and other German strategists on how best to stop the coming assault.

Rundstedt, 68 years old and nearing retirement, had never believed in fixed defenses such as the Atlantic Wall. He would quote Fredrick the Great, saying, "He who would defend all defends nothing." It was Rundstedt's master planning that had enabled Nazi troops to outflank the French Maginot Line—a barrier of underground fortifications designed to stop a German invasion of France. Rundstedt had simply sent mobile troops around the Maginot Line through neutral countries and over it, using paratroops.

Rundstedt believed the Allies would penetrate the Atlantic Wall just as easily. His plan for stopping the Allies called for keeping large reserves of panzers and infantry in a centrally located area of France. When the invasion came, these troops would be rushed to the coast to combat the Allies. This plan was supported by most of the German general staff in the west including General Heinz Guderian, Hitler's personal tank expert.

Rommel disagreed. He believed the invasion had to be smashed in the water before the Allies could even get on the beach. Rommel, who had learned a painful lesson about Allied air power in Africa, knew that British and American planes would demolish any reserves trying to reach the coast.

By early 1944 the Allies virtually ruled the skies over Europe. Bombing raids over Germany by 3,000 Allied warplanes was becoming commonplace. Luftwaffe (German Air Force) units, the ones that were left, were desperately needed on the Russian and Italian fronts. By spring of 1944 the Germans had trouble even sending photo-taking reconnaisance flights over Britain. Most were shot down.

Rommel argued that if the Allies were allowed to gain the smallest foothold on the French coast, their strength in men and material would build up so rapidly they would be impossible to dislodge. Rommel's plan called for digging panzer and infantry reserves into the beach defenses or just behind them.

Rommel had a tough time trying to convince Rundstedt and the other generals in the west that his plan was the only one that would succeed. Many of the generals under Rommel were veterans of the war in Russia where the Luftwaffe controlled the air. These generals believed they would be able to move troops and panzers from one end of the battlefield to the other as they had done in Russia.

Rommel told them that against the British and Americans, German mobile warfare was obsolete. "The war will be won or lost on the beaches," Rommel said. "We'll have only one chance to stop the enemy and that's while he's in the water."

This argument would go on right up until the invasion. In the meantime, Rommel set to work strengthening the Atlantic Wall. Rommel had made an inspection tour of the defenses after taking command and had found them totally inadequate.

Hitler had put an enormous responsibility on Rommel's shoulders. He told him the whole future of Germany and Nazism depended on the outcome of the invasion battle. "When the enemy invades in the west, it will be the moment of decision in this war and the moment must turn to our advantage."

Rommel would work tirelessly over the next six months creating what he would call the "Death Zone."

A large German long range gun points to the sky from its curious emplacement which Berlin stated was in position on the Channel coast.

Anti-invasion guns dot a French beach along the English Channel.

CHAPTER III: *Death Zone*

Following his first inspection trip, Rommel was shocked at the weaknesses he found in Hitler's much-publicized Atlantic Wall which was more like a flimsy barricade.

Rundstedt had been less than enthusiastic about strengthening the coastal defenses. His plan was to wait until after the Allies had landed, then mass his troops and attack.

Rommel also discovered that although he had over a million men "on paper," many of the German units had only half or a third as many troops as they were supposed to have. For the last two years, the Nazi high command had been taking full divisions from the west and using them to replace units in Russia. In exchange, divisions that had been horribly decimated fighting the Russians were sent to France.

As the war drained German manpower some of their western front infantry divisions contained old men and young boys and others were made of "volunteers" from captive nations—Poles, Hungarians, Czechs, Rumanians, Yugoslavs and even Russians and Mongolians. These were men who had decided it was better to fight for the Germans than to die in a concentration camp.

Despite the obvious language problems and the questionable loyalty of these troops, they were commanded by a backbone of highly-trained, battle-tested German officers.

And supporting Rommel's Army Group B were six crack panzer divisions. However, these powerful tank units were still based far from the coast. Rommel continued to argue they be placed at the Wall. "Reserves will never get up to the point of attack and it's foolish to even consider them. Everything we have must be on the coast," Rommel would say.

Though there was little Rommel could do to bolster his manpower, there was still much that could be done to improve the coastal defenses.

Slave laborers, paid French workers and German troops worked around the clock on the Atlantic Wall. During the six months leading up to the invasion over half a million persons dug communications trenches, laid mines, strung barbed wire, erected beach obstacles and built fortified positions of steel and concrete.

Rommel was everywhere along the Wall. Each day he would inspect a different sector, praising or criticizing, whatever the situation called for. He was constantly designing new types of obstacles, barriers and explosive devices, using materials he could find on hand.

Millions of tons of concrete were used to build new bombproof gun emplacements, bunkers and underground rooms. This caused a cement shortage in Europe. When Rommel could not get enough concrete fast enough, he built his own concrete plants at the coast. When his construction projects required more and more electrical power, Rommel's work crews set up new power plants near the coast. When there was not enough fuel for the power plants, Rommel reopened abandoned coal mines and dug his own.

General Wilhelm Meise, Rommel's military engineering adviser, called Rommel the "greatest engineer of the Second World War."

The master blueprint for France's coastal defenses drawn up by Rommel was a six-mile-deep strip running the length of the beach called the "Death Zone."

This lethal barrier would begin in the sea and stretch, in some areas, as far as seven or eight miles inland.

The first defensive devices of the Death Zone an invader would encounter were nautical mines, strung out in the Channel to sink ships and boats. Closer to shore, the next horror that landing craft, ships and amphibious vehicles would meet was a huge array of wooden, steel and concrete obstacles—most crowned with mines.

Some obstacles were built from scrap steel salvaged from railroad trestles destroyed by Allied bombing. These were welded together to form huge triangular shaped forms to stop tanks and boats. Other obstacles were large cone or pyramid-shaped blocks of concrete.

The simplest were heavy wooden posts driven into the beach, topped with mines, others with jagged plates of steel—called "can openers"—to rip the bottom out of landing craft.

At high tide, these obstacles would be covered by the sea and would present the greatest danger to the invader. But at low tide, the obstacles, even though visible, would still stop or slow down an amphibious assault.

On the beaches were row after row of barbed wire and more concrete tank barriers. On the rises and cliffs above the beach were the fortifications. These housed long-range guns that could fire at ships at sea and smaller artillery that could pound the beaches. There were pillboxes protecting machine gun positions and bunkers for tanks and anti-tank guns. There were fortified holes for mortars and multiple rocket launchers that could hurl dozens of deadly projectiles at the invader. In some areas there were even automatic flame throwers that could be triggered from a distant bunker to set grassy areas aflame when the invasion troops reached them.

The Germans, in some sectors, had lethal devices called "Goliaths." These were driverless, remote controlled, miniature tanks that could be sent down to the beach carrying 1,000 pounds of explosives where they would detonate among troops.

Behind the beaches, every open field that could be used by the Allies for paratroop or glider landings was studded with wooden posts and planted with mines. The wooden posts, nicknamed "Rommel's asparagus" by the Allies, were designed to demolish gliders and the soldiers inside them as they swooped in at 100 m.p.h. Any glider that landed between the posts would trip wires attached to mines on top of the posts, detonating them. The Germans also buried anti-personnel mines in these fields to kill troops who survived the other obstacles.

Many fields of the region were low lying and the Germans simply flooded them with water from rivers or the sea. Paratroops landing here would drown or at least be slowed down.

Rommel, who had learned the value of mines in Africa, had millions of them planted everywhere inside the Death Zone. When he couldn't get his hands on enough mines fast enough, Rommel grabbed warehouses full of captured French explosives and set up his own plants.

He also devised a way to use 1,200,000 obsolete artillery shells. His invention was called the "Nutcracker" mine. An artillery shell was placed in a concrete housing with the tip facing upward. Over the tip of the shell was attached a wooden or metal plank. When this device was placed underwater, a ship, boat or vehicle brushing over it would push the plank down causing the shell to hit a firing pin which would detonate it.

The feverish work along the coast and Rommel's

presence raised the spirits of Army Group B. The fact that something positive was being done to stop the coming Allied assault boosted morale.

Once picturesque beaches were now covered with a growing ugly rash of steel, concrete and barbed wire. But these scenes were not ugly to the men who had to defend this coast—they were comforting sights.

Rommel knew these defenses by themselves could not stop the gigantic army that would assault them. But he believed the Wall would slow down an invasion long enough to concentrate forces behind it and destroy the invader. His main worry now was how to talk Hitler into putting the reserves on the beach.

Meanwhile, just 100 miles away in England, men were preparing an onslaught against Hitler's Fortress Europe that would make a mockery of the German Army and the so-called "master race."

German Field Marshal General Rommel reviews the crew of a German coastal battery on the English Channel coast sometime in 1944.

CHAPTER IV: *Bolero*

The English Channel stretches for 300 miles and varies from 20 to 100 miles in width. The often storm-tossed body of water separates the British Isles from the rest of Europe.

In 1066, when Europe was made up of dozens of small kingdoms, William I of Normandy invaded Britain from France with an armed force. William's Norman troops defeated the Saxons who had controlled Britain and the huge island became part of Normandy.

The date, 1066, probably the only date every Englishman has memorized, was the last time in nine centuries that Britain would be invaded.

Over the years the Normans, Saxons and other peoples of England merged to form one nation. Over the centuries the people of England were allowed to develop separately from the rest of Europe. The Channel protected them.

And because of the Channel, the people of England learned to become seafarers in order to trade with the rest of the world. In the sixteenth century Britain emerged as the major sea power of the world. This sea power enabled England to explore the entire globe over the next few hundred years and to colonize much of it. The English acquired much wealth from their colonies as well as raw materials and products for trading with the rest of the world.

In 1588 Britain became the target of its chief world rival, Spain. King Philip II sent a huge mass of warships to invade England. They were defeated by the English fleet under Sir Francis Drake, by a devastating ocean storm and by the Channel.

In 1805, after Napoleon had conquered most of Europe, it was the Channel that again spared England from invasion and enabled her ultimately to defeat the French Army.

And in 1940, with the rest of Europe under Nazi rule, the Channel was still there to protect England. Depsite all the machines of modern warfare, Hitler could only gaze across the choppy stretch of water from France at the last bastion of freedom in Europe. As long as Britain controlled the sea and the air a German invasion would be doomed.

As early as March 1941, nine months before the United States officially entered World War II, American, British and Canadian leaders met secretly to discuss how to defeat the Axis powers now rampaging across half the continents of the world.

It was decided that Germany was the most powerful and dangerous nation in the Axis, Japan was a secondary worry and that Italy would be only a minor problem. Therefore, it was agreed that when the U.S. entered the war, its first task would be helping Britain to destroy the German military and to liberate Europe. This would be done by an invasion of France following a huge buildup of troops and war material in England. The invasion would be code-named Overlord, the buildup Bolero.

In these days it was a certainty that the U.S. would soon be fighting the Germans. American manufacturers were developing and producing weapons and ships for the British.

U.S. cargo ships escorted by U.S. naval vessels were bringing supplies to the beleagured island across the Atlantic. Many of them were attacked and some were sunk by German submarines. And German U-boats were being sunk right in American waters where they waited to prey on British shipping moving in and out of U.S. ports.

America finally entered the war on December 7, 1941, after the Japanese attacked Pearl Harbor, Hawaii.

Four days later, Hitler declared war on the United States in a speech in which he described American soldiers as "a bunch of rowdies" who did not have the guts for full-scale war. Hitler's absurd racial theories convinced him that the U.S.—composed of people of many extractions and cultures—could not produce troops capable of standing up to the "Master Race."

Rewriting and updating the original British cross-channel strategy, Allies came up with an outline for coastal assault in early 1942. Brigadier General Dwight D. Eisenhower, chief of the War Plans Division in Washington, won approval for his plan from President Franklin D. Roosevelt, Secretary of War Henry L. Stimson and Army Chief of Staff General George C. Marshall.

As early as October 1941 British military planners had been creating amphibious training centers, developing devices and tactics for invasion, and had been collecting intelligence data on the German-held Atlantic coast.

The British had also been developing ships and boats for landing heavy equipment and troops on beaches since 1938. The LST (Landing Ship Tank), work horse of the D-Day amphibious fleet, was born when British improvisers cut the bow out of a shallow-draft oil tanker and replaced the bow with ramps on hinges. This vessel could move through shallow water right up to the beach, drop its ramp, and out would pour combat-ready soldiers, tanks, vehicles or artillery.

Before the U.S. even entered the war, American

shipbuilders were producing a variety of landing ships and craft from British blueprints. When America entered the war, production was increased ten-fold to meet needs in North Africa and for the island-hopping American campaign against the Japanese.

In the meantime, British shipyards were turning out the smaller version of the LST, the LCT (Landing Craft Tank). Unlike the LST, the LCT could travel only short distances and was not truly seaworthy.

From these two basic prototypes, the LST and LCT, an endless variety of amphibious landing ships and boats was developed. Each had its specialized job.

Some were:

LSH, Landship Ship Headquarters—These ships were the floating command posts. Field commanders would direct the battle from these armored communications centers until the command staff landed on the beach.

LSI, Landing Ship Infantry—Many of these ships were converted passenger liners which carried small assault landing craft in place of lifeboats. They could steam to invasion area, lay several miles offshore, and launch their troop-filled landing craft.

LCG, Landing Craft Gun—These support craft would not land on the beach but would carry an array of weapons for neutralizing enemy defenses on shore. Some carried two 4.7-inch naval guns and lighter weapons. Some carried anti-aircraft guns, heavy machine guns, mortars and rockets.

Fighter Direction Tenders—These LST's were used to control fighter aircraft supporting troops on the beach and providing air cover for the fleet.

Landing Barges—These motorized barges and rafts carried landing craft, anti-aircraft batteries and later were used to ferry across locomotives and railroad cars.

Various facets of cross-channel warfare were

being tested against the German-held coast in small-scale commando raids. Three weeks after the British had been kicked off the continent by Hitler's blitzkreig, small groups of armed Englishmen began raiding the French coast.

In the spring of 1942 British commandos raided and destroyed a major section of the German naval base at Saint-Nazaire. Then in August of that year, a force of 6,000 British and Canadian troops and some American Rangers crossed the Channel and hit the French port of Dieppe. Over 900 Allied servicemen were killed and 2,000 were taken prisoner by the Germans.

The assault involved putting infantry and armor ashore from 250 landing craft and ships. The operation was a test of new amphibious techniques and machines. It was also conducted to see if a fortified port could be captured by a seaborne assault by commandos.

One thing the Allies learned from this bloodbath was that in order to knock out shore defenses fast enough, many tanks and artillery pieces had to be landed with the first troops on the beach. Some landing craft would also be modified so that tanks and field pieces could fire at the shore while still at sea.

Advanced planning for Overlord began in 1943. To carry out the operation 3,000,000 men would have to be trained, equipped, and kept supplied. The invasion would ultimately involve 3,500,000 Allied servicemen, more than half of them American.

Overlord planners began looking for the best possible landing areas along the Atlantic Wall. On the surface, the Dieppe-Calais coast seemed the most obvious choice for a beachhead. It had wide beaches and was closest to England. But the problem with this area, as the Dieppe raid had shown, was that it was too well defended. The German 15th Army, the main strength of Rommel's Army Group B, was stationed in this area, hidden behind massive fortifications.

To the west, down the French coast from Dieppe, was Normandy and the Cherbourg Peninsula. This area was fortified but did not contain as many Wehrmacht troops or panzers as Dieppe-Calais.

Normandy's beaches were adequate for landing an invasion force. Inland, there were wide, open fields for paratroop and glider landings. The area was within range of Allied ships and craft and could also be covered from the air by English-based fighters and bombers. The deep-water port of Cherbourg was also in the area. Once captured, the landing of troops and equipment could be increased rapidly.

Another feature of Normandy's topography which interested Overlord strategists was the way in which Norman farmers divided their fields. Pastures and cultivated areas in this ancient French province were separated by hedgerows. These were borders of trees, stone walls, boulders and thick shrubs built up over the centures. It was very difficult for tank and mobile units to operate effectively in this area.

As a result, the Allies reasoned the Germans would find it hard to move their panzers to the beachhead in time to stop the invasion. German armor and reinforcements would have to follow known roads where they would be targets for Allied warplanes.

Another reason the Normandy area was picked for invasion was simply for surprise since the Germans expected the Allies to land in the Calais area.

To assure success, the Allies would need to gather every bit of information they could about Normandy. Planners turned to old road maps, travel magazines, post cards and nautical charts. English citizens who had toured Normandy were sought out and questioned. At the same time, specially-trained Allied agents were put ashore at night in Normandy to check the hardness of the beaches to see if they could take the weight of tanks and other heavy vehicles.

Reconnaisance planes took thousands of photos right up to the date of the invasion as Normandy's coastal defenses multiplied. Before the invasion, Allied tacticians would be able to produce maps showing every path, road, stone wall, anti-tank ditch, machine gun position, rifle pit, gun battery, minefield, beach obstacle and strand of barbed wire.

With this information, Allied bombers would know exactly where to drop their deadly loads and when the day came, Allied warships would know which areas to blast with their heavy naval guns.

Ground troop commanders would at least have a short time to plan how to lead their soldiers around the most lethal defensive positions. Soliders would have some idea where the minefields and barbed wire were concentrated.

By the fall of 1943 southwest England was an anthill of activity. Camps had sprung up for newly arriving American troops. Ammunition and supply depots began to grow and more than 160 new airbases had been built since the Americans arrived. Training centers for the GI's were set up along the coast.

In December 1943 General Dwight D. Eisenhower was named Supreme Allied Commander of the invasion forces. "Ike," as he was known to soldiers and presidents alike, had been in charge of highly successful amphibious operations in North Africa which had led to the defeat of Rommel's Afrika Korps. The 54-year-old Kansas native was a graduate of West Point and, on the surface, was a charming, diplomatic organizer who could weld American and British forces into one great army.

But he was also a great strategist who painstakingly covered every tiny detail to insure an operation's success. He had proved this not only in Africa but during the invasion of Sicily and Italy.

Much work had been done by the time Ike took

command but there was still an enormous task ahead. Three different factors could make or break the invasion.

If the Germans could gather 20 or more divisions to hit the beachhead in the first few days, they could push the Allies back into the sea. Despite accelerated production in England and the U.S., there would not be as many landing craft and ships as Ike would like. The invasion fleet would be able to put about nine divisions ashore in one day. After that, the Allies would be able to land one division per day plus supplies for the beachhead.

Eisenhower also worried about the weather. If a storm blew up after the first day, the troops on the beach could be cut off from supplies enabling the Wehrmacht to defeat them.

The third big worry was secrecy. If the Germans learned where the Allies were going to land, they could mass troops and panzers in the area to assure an Allied defeat.

Britons and Americans had been working on the problem of secrecy for some time. There was no possible way to hide the vast numbers of troops and huge quantities of military hardware piling up in southern England, or hide row after row of LST's and warships beginning to clog England's Channel ports. But the Allies could try to fool the Germans into thinking all this military might was going to be directed somewhere other than Normandy.

This elaborate scheme would be code-named Fortitude.

CHAPTER V: *Fortitude*

In late 1943 and the first six months of 1944, Allied intelligence officers perpetrated a gigantic hoax on the Germans under the code name Fortitude.

Fortitude consisted of false information fed to the Germans by radio, by spies, by diplomats, in the press and through resistance groups in occupied countries. Each bit of information was designed to confuse the enemy and lead him away from the site of the forthcoming invasion, Normandy.

Fortitude North, based on fiction, was a nonexistent plan to invade Norway by an equally nonexistent "Fourth Army." Fourth Army consisted of a few squads of radio personnel and communication equipment. The Germans, who monitored much Allied radio traffic, picked up thousands of phony messages of the Fourth Army. These signals hinted that the invasion would come in Norway some time in July. In addition, minesweeping and antisubmarine operations were conducted off Norway, dummy gliders were parked in Scottish fields and messages were broadcast in Norwegian.

Fortitude South was designed to deceive the Germans into thinking the invasion would come at Calais, France. Since most of the Wehrmacht already believed Calais would be the target, Fortitude South was devoured hook, line and sinker by the Germans.

In southeastern Britain, directly across the Channel from Calais, large quantities of obsolete aircraft along with inflatable rubber dummy tanks were arranged in fields to fool the few German reconnaisance planes allowed to penetrate Britain's air cover. Loudspeakers were installed in these areas to play recordings of aircraft warming up and other noises to fool German spies who might be nearby.

To further mislead the enemy 24-hour-a-day radio traffic created the impression that a huge army group was located in Dover under the command of the highly-respected American tank genius, Lieutenant General George S. Patton. The Germans were led to believe that Patton would spearhead the main assault on Calais. Inflatable rubber and plywood landing craft were placed along the Dover coast.

At the same time, to further confuse German intelligence, spies were told to circulate the rumor in Paris that Allied production of landing craft would not be fast enough for an Atlantic invasion and, instead, the assault would come on France's Mediterranean coast. This made some sense because defenses were weaker in the Mediterranean and there was an abundance of deepwater ports to handle large ships.

Then Holland became the target of Fortitude. The Allied command placed ads in newspapers for Dutch-speaking radio announcers. Dutch underground agents were even briefed about plans for a Holland invasion. One Dutch agent was captured by the Germans and tortured until he revealed what he knew. Apparently the phony plan fooled the Germans for a time because they flooded 5,000 square miles of Holland in April 1944 to slow any Allied invasion there.

One of the more bizarre deceptions was code named Columba. Hundreds of homing pigeons in boxes were parachuted throughout the Calais area and in Holland and Belgium. Notes attached to the birds said that when they were released they would fly back to their lofts in England and deliver any information on the Germans the finder had to offer. Few made it back. Many were eaten by the farmers who found them. But since they had been parachuted around the Calais area, the Calais invasion deception was strengthened.

Shortly after Ike was named supreme commander, British Field Marshal Sir Bernard Montgomery was chosen to lead Allied ground forces on D-Day. Montgomery, who was then conducting an attack on Italy, had to be brought to England to begin planning and organizing. His absence would be noted by the Germans.

In May 1944, with the invasion only a month away, a British actor who closely resembled Montgomery was recruited to impersonate the famous field marshal. He was sent to the British military base at Gibraltar in the Mediterranean where he strutted around the base for the next month fooling even the British personnel.

Through their agents in Spain, the Germans soon found out "Monty" was at Gibraltar. Hitler was convinced that Montgomery was there to plan operations. As a result, Hitler decided that at least seven Wehrmacht divisions would have to remain stationed in southern France.

Another important part of Fortitude was the costly but convincing deception carried out by Allied bombers. Since railroads would be one of the chief means of bringing troops and supplies to Normandy by the Germans, Allied air power had to start knocking out tracks, marshaling yards and railroad bridges months before the invasion.

To keep the Germans from learning the site of the assault, the Allied air forces were required to bomb two targets elsewhere for every target they bombed in Normandy. This, probably more than anything else, convinced the German high command that Calais would be the area of assault.

Besides this deception, the soldiers and sailors of D-Day would owe much to the American and British air forces. The pilots and crews of the bombers and fighters would begin their assault months before the surface invasion. And, as was proved in North Africa, Italy and in the Pacific, the ultimate weapon was air power.

CHAPTER VI: *Pointblank*

"It was all a question of air force, air force, and air force again." —*Comment made by German Field Marshal Gerd von Rundstedt on the German defeat at Normandy.*

Over the years since D-Day most historians—American, British and German—have agreed that air power was the single most decisive force that won not only Normandy for the Allies but the war.

Allied strategists early in the war knew if a cross-Channel invasion of France was to succeed, the German Luftwaffe would first have to be blasted and chased from the skies of western Europe. If the Allies controlled, the air they could keep Luftwaffe war planes from wreaking havoc on Allied beach landings and on the huge naval force that would be in the Channel.

Air superiority for the Allies would also mean German ground troops and installations would be without Luftwaffe air cover. There would be no German fighter planes to protect beach defenses and guns, lines of communications, masses of troops and panzers from Allied air attack. The Wehrmacht would be pinned down, unable to move units in the open during daylight hours without heavy losses.

In June 1943 the combined bomber offensive began from bases in southern England, aimed at the heart of Germany. The main objective of this operation, code-named Pointblank, was to destroy the German air force.

Pointblank would be carried out by the U.S. Eighth Air Force, the British Royal Air Force Bomber Command, and later by the U.S. Ninth Air Force and the British Second Tactical Air Force.

Eighth Air Force and the British Bomber Command were strategic air forces, meaning their missions had long-range effects on the outcome of the war. These units were composed of long-range bombers and escort fighters. Their primary target was German industry.

The British Second Tactical Air Force and the U.S. Ninth were tactical units, meaning their role was more concerned with short-range and immediate tasks, including the air defense of England and attacks on targets within 400 miles of their bases. These units were composed of fighters, fighter-bombers and medium and light bombers. Their primary targets were German military bases and communication lines in France.

From June to December 1943 Pointblank did not go well for the Allies, especially the Americans. Their bomber forces were small and new to combat. And the Allies had only short-range escort fighters whose pilots could not follow the big B-17, B-24, Lancaster and Halifax bombers deep into Nazi territory. Bombing raids had to be limited in size because of heavy losses.

Between January and June 1944 Eighth Air Force increased its fighter and bomber strength by 50 percent and Ninth Air Force by 500 percent. At the same time the British also added more planes and personnel to the RAF Bomber Command and to Second Tactical Air Force.

This tremendous expansion of air power began at the same time that large quantities of the new long-range escort fighters—P-47's and P-51's—began to arrive at British air bases from the United States. These fighters could protect the bombers all the way into Germany and back. By early 1944 Allied air power outnumbered the Luftwaffe. This gave the Allies the opportunity to train their inexperienced airmen on the job with fewer losses.

The bombing attacks were aimed at aircraft production facilities and Luftwaffe air fields as well as war material plants and later the German synthetic fuel production facilities. The primary goal of many of these raids was to provoke the Luftwaffe fighter force into the air where they could be destroyed by Allied fighters.

The peak of intensity of this air war came in February and March 1944 when American and British fighters dealt such a hard blow to the Luftwaffe fighter force it never recovered. In those two months Germany lost most of her best pilots.

As the year 1944 progressed Allied escort fighters began taking an offensive rather than defensive role. The P-47's and P-51's would fly ahead of the bombers seeking out enemy fighters to attack in the air or on the ground.

At the same time, the Allied tactical air forces began chasing and destroying Luftwaffe aircraft over France, Holland, Luxembourg and Belgium. Tactical bombers and fighters smashed Nazi air bases in these countries again and again.

One result of both the strategic and tactical offenses was that the Germans had to pull their air force closer and closer to Germany. By the time D-Day arrived, they would have few serviceable air fields left within range of the Normandy beaches. In fact, the Luftwaffe had been so badly mauled and demoralized that during the two weeks before the invasion it sent no reconnaisance flights over England to photograph the build-up there.

So, by D-Day, Allied air power had succeeded in its most important job of wiping the German air force from the sky. The second big job for the airmen was called the Transportation Bombing Program.

One advantage the Germans would have when the invasion began was the ability to build up forces at the beach faster than the Allies. The Wehrmacht could bring in reinforcements using the vast highway and railroad network of northwest Europe. If the Nazis could bring enough troops and panzers to the Normandy coast fast enough, they could defeat the invasion and turn the whole tide of the war. The Allies could only reinforce themselves by ship and boat. A few days of bad weather and a German victory would be possible.

The only answer to this problem was for the Allied air forces to destroy and damage as many railroad and highway systems as possible leading into Normandy. The German forces in the invasion area would have to be isolated from communication and reinforcement.

Allied leaders decided that not only would the Normandy battle field have to be isolated, but also, the railroad system running from Germany across Belgium and northern France would have to be temporarily rendered useless.

A few months before D-Day Allied bombers began pounding railroad centers, marshaling yards, bridges, rail repair facilities, tunnels, freight cars and locomotives. The raids stretched from Germany to Normandy. In the four months before D-Day, train traffic between Germany and France dropped by 70 percent. More than 1,600 Nazi troop and supply trains were destroyed.

The Ninth Air Force went after the highway and railroad bridges leading to Normandy. To confuse the enemy as to where the invasion was to take place, for every bombing mission around Normandy the tactical squadrons were forced to make two bombing runs in the Calais area. And to further protect the invasion forces the Allies began bombing German coastal radar stations in early May. These raids destroyed 72 percent of German coastal radar facilities.

As D-Day neared, the Allied air force was called on to begin a systematic pounding of Rommel's Death Zone along the French coast. This was made possible by the lack of Luftwaffe opposition and by the fact that more and more German anti-aircraft batteries were being sent back to Germany because of the massive bombing there.

As huge a job as the Allied air forces had, the naval forces of Britain and the United States would have just as big a role. Though their jobs would be far different than that of the airmen, they would be just as vital. This huge task would include transporting about 160,000 men in one day from England to France, along with all the supplies and heavy weapons they would need. In the following weeks, if all went as planned, another million would be carried by ship and boat across the Channel. This operation was called Neptune.

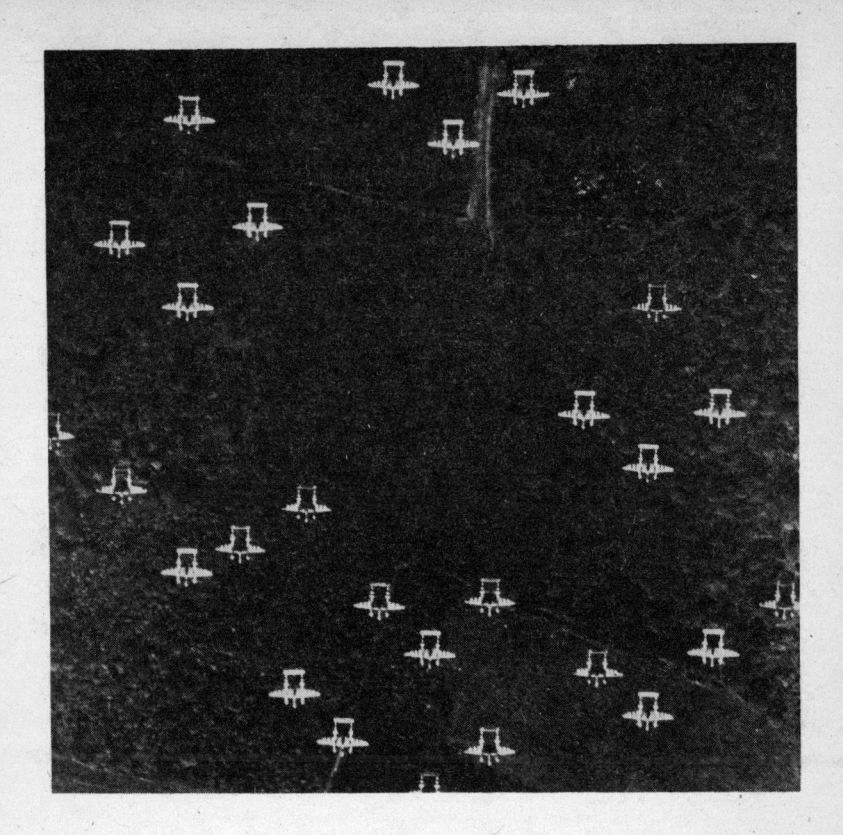

Wearing their striped "invasion insignia", Lockheed Lightnings of a photo reconnaissance group strike out toward France on D-Day. The picture, taken from a P-38 (F-5) camera ship flying above the formation, shows only a portion of the photo group.

CHAPTER VII: *Neptune*

"The effects of heavy naval bombardment are so powerful that an operation either with infantry or armored formations is impossible in an area commanded by this rapid firing artillery." —*Message from Field Marshal Erwin Rommel to Adolph Hitler on June 11, 1944, concerning Allied naval gun fire.*

Germany had one thing going for it in the first years of war that almost brought the powerful naval force of Great Britain to its knees—the U-boat.

For the first three years of war German submarines terrorized the seas in a battle of increasing destruction for Allied shipping. In 1942 U-boats sank 7,699,000 tons, well over 1,000 British and American tankers, cargo ships and naval vessels. These ships were vital in keeping the island of Britain alive as well as supplying Allied troops fighting the Axis in North Africa.

President Roosevelt and British Prime Minister Churchill agreed at the beginning of 1943 that unless the Nazi U-boats were stopped, an invasion of Fortress Europe could never take place. The German submarine force, commanded by Admiral Karl

Doenitz, was sinking ships as fast as America and England could build them. Something had to be done. This struggle was called the Battle of the Atlantic.

The Allied air force was called upon to bomb the German U-boat bases at several French ports on the Atlantic coast. These submarine pens, as they were called, were tunneled into cliffs, river banks and under docks at sea level. They were so heavily protected by concrete that after 11,000 tons of high explosive and 8,000 tons of fire bombs, the Allied air force admitted the pens were invulnerable from air attack.

It was the Allied navy's turn. Using a variety of new techniques and equipment, the tide turned rapidly against the Germans. To better protect shipping convoys British and American naval support groups were formed. These were miniature battle fleets that usually included an aircraft carrier and would escort large lines of vessels across the ocean. A radio location system was set up to monitor U-boat radio traffic. This helped navy planes and destroyers to find and sink the U-boats. New radar equipment located Nazi subs. A device was developed that enabled ships to hurl several depth charges into the sea at one time, and the depth charges themselves were improved.

Up to this time there had been what was known as the "air gap," an area of the Atlantic which was out of range of Allied anti-submarine aircraft. It was in this area that Admiral Doenitz had placed many of his 400 U-boats. The coming of longer-range aircraft made it possible to reduce this "air gap."

In March 1943 the Allies lost 627,000 tons of shipping to the U-boats. In April this fell dramatically to 260,000 tons and the Allies sank 41 U-boats—the worst single loss yet for Admiral Doenitz.

Before this time, the German navy was losing about one U-boat for each 100,000 tons of Allied shipping sunk. This was a loss the Germans could afford. By May 1943 the ratio had changed to one U-boat lost for every 10,000 tons of Allied shipping. The Germans simply could not afford this rate of loss.

The U-boat menace would continue throughout the war but never on the scale of pre-May 1943. Doenitz withdrew most of his submarines from the Atlantic before all of them were sunk. For the rest of the war they would confine themselves to harrassing naval forces all over the world, but would never again be a serious threat. The British and Americans had won the Battle of the Atlantic.

Now the Allied navy would be called upon for another battle—Normandy. The naval operations of Overlord were code-named Neptune. The tasks of the American and British navies would be huge and unending.

On D-Day 160,000 men plus millions of tons of supplies and combat equipment would have to be delivered from England to France and unloaded on beaches or in shallow water. All this would have to be accomplished under the massed firepower of Rommel's shore defenses.

Neptune would involve nearly 7,000 ships and landing craft of the Allied navy. Landing ships, landing craft and barges to carry troops, heavy weapons and vehicles would total 4,000. More than 220 destroyers, sloops, frigates, corvettes, armed trawlers and patrol craft would escort the landing fleet.

To bombard the concrete fortifications of Rommel's Death Zone were the devastating guns of six battleships, two monitors with huge 15-inch guns, 23 cruisers, two gunboats, and more than 100 destroyers. In addition to this firepower were hundreds of small landing craft fitted with a variety of guns and rockets for firing onto the shore.

Almost 300 minesweepers would be used to clear

the Channel and the coastal waters off Normandy, aided by 500 light coastal craft. Fifty-eight armed vessels would be needed to patrol approaches to the invasion against U-boats. And there would be 500 other ships for a variety of uses including dock ships, tugs, salvage vessels, survey ships, telephone cable ships, mooring ships and buoy-laying vessels.

There were ships which could make smoke to hide the fleet from the enemy. There were ships that would lay an underwater pipeline to carry gasoline and diesel fuel from England to Normandy beneath the choppy Channel. There were also 800 merchant ships for carrying supplies and ammunition, tankers for carrying fuel and drinking water. And there were hospital ships and small craft which would rescue pilots, soldiers and sailors as their planes were shot down or their ships sunk.

Since it might be a month or more before Allied troops captured the deepwater port of Cherbourg, some facility would be required to unload deep-draft cargo ships that could not unload at the beach or in shallow water, including the 7,000-ton Liberty ships, backbone of the American merchant fleet.

The British developed and built artificial harbors code named Mulberries. These consisted first of huge hollow concrete rectangles that could be towed on barges across the Channel. These would be dropped in the Channel off Normandy end to end to form a semicircle off the beach. The semicircle would be reinforced by sinking obsolete freighters in line with the rectangles. This wall, called a breakwater, would stop or slow down waves and tides that could interfere with the unloading of ships.

Inside the breakwater would be more submerged concrete structures with floating docks attached to them. Running from the docks to the beach were floating roadways on pontoons. As the invasion progressed, it would be up to the Allied navy to tow three of these massive contraptions to Normandy and assemble them.

Some of the concrete caissons, as the rectangles were called, were 200 feet long, 55 feet wide, 60 feet high and weighed 12,000,000 pounds. The three Mulberries would require 213 caissons, 23 floating piers, 55 blockships sunk with the caissons and 10 miles of floating roadway.

Provided the Allies gained a beachhead on Normandy, they would have to be supplied daily and increasing amounts of troops would have to be landed to expand the beachhead into a full-blown battle front. So Neptune would not be a short operation but would last 30 days or more until the port of Cherbourg could be captured and made ready for use.

This colossal assembly of ships, the largest in history, was jammed into every harbor, inlet and cove of southern England. When the time came, the armada would move into the Channel and assemble off the Isle of Wight into two task forces.

The Eastern Task Force would carry British and Canadian forces to three Normandy beaches stretching from the Orne River to the seaside town of Port-en-Bessin. Two British and one Canadian division would form the first assault in this sector.

The Western Task Force would transport three U.S. divisions for the initial assault on two beaches located between Port-en-Besslin and the Cotentin Peninsula.

These two task forces together were further broken down into five assault forces, each assault force representing one of the five beaches to be attacked.

Clearing the way for these thousands of ships were the minesweepers. It was known there was a German mine barrier running down the middle of the Channel plus other fields of mines near the French coast. In the largest operation of its kind in history, the minesweepers would have to sweep, and mark with buoys, 10 shipping channels into the Normandy coast. Each assault force would have two channels, one for slow traffic and one for fast. This system of mine-swept lanes was known as the "spout."

Next, the minesweepers would have to search out and clear areas off the assault beaches where the bombardment ships could anchor to blast the shore.

To protect this gigantic array of shipping would be groups of destroyers and armed patrol craft forming several lines on each of the flanks and to the seaward side of the invasion. Three British aircraft carriers would be stationed in a line south of England to launch an anti-submarine screen across the western approaches to the Channel. This was in case any of Admiral Doenitz' surviving U-boats came out of the Atlantic.

Allied naval tacticians were worried that once much of the fleet was at anchor, small German torpedo boats could try to slip out of the French ports of Cherbourg or Le Havre and penetrate the fleet defenses by hugging the coastline until they were within torpedo range of the big ships. To guard against such tactics the British laid extensive minefields in the waters outside any French port they considered dangerous.

In addition to this protection, there would be thousands of Allied aircraft in the skies over the invasion day and night. These airmen would constantly be scanning the horizon for the Luftwaffe as well as watching the sea for German U-boats or surface vessels.

The Allied navy would not only have a huge job on D-Day, it would have to follow an exact timetable. Then it would have to supply and resupply the invasion with men and war material until the beachhead was expanded to include the port of Cherbourg.

General Omar Bradley, leader of American invasion forces, said before D-Day, "You can almost always force an invasion but you can't always make it stick." It would be up to the navy to "make it stick."

Not only would the Allied bombardment fleet use its big guns against the shore, it would also use them to support the soldiers as they moved inland into the green hedgerow country of Normandy. The Germans would be amazed at the distance these guns could fire. The British battleship Rodney, after the invasion began, would maul and terrorize a German panzer unit 17 miles inland from the beach.

But despite all the help from the skies and from the sea that the ground troops would get, the foot soldier, the tankers, the paratroopers and the artillerymen would still have to take Normandy away from the Germans.

Picture taken on board the Captain Class Frigate H.M.S. Holmes when she formed part of the escort to the Navy's big ships off Le Harve during their bombardment of enemy positions on the Normandy coast on June 6th 1944.

A puff of black smoke blows away from the guns of the USS Arkansas as the mighty battleship lays down a tremendous barrage against German installations on the beach area of France, in support to the Allied ground forces who stormed the Norman beaches.

CHAPTER VIII: *Okay. We'll Go!*

On May 17, 1944, General Eisenhower informed Allied leaders that the invasion would take place on June 5, 6, or 7. These dates were decided on because of two factors important to landing troops: the moon and the tide.

Landings from the sea had to take place at low tide so that Rommel's beach obstacles would be exposed. This tide would have to be during daylight hours so that naval personnel steering the ships and boats could find their assigned beaches. This would have to be followed by another low tide, the same day, also during daylight, so a followup landing could be made.

For paratroop and glider landings, which would take place in the dark early morning hours before the beach landings, moonlight was needed. However, it would have to be a moon that did not rise until about 1 a.m. so that darkness would hide the operation until the gliders and transport planes were over the drop zones.

Calculating all these needs had produced the three days in June that the invasion could be launched at its earliest.

For the men who would make up the invasion, this cold, rainy British spring was filled with practice, practice and more practice. English beaches had been converted into replicas of Rommel's Death Zone and sailors and soldiers went through endless rehearsals of beaching and unloading landing craft.

Army combat engineers and Navy underwater demolition specialists practiced their dangerous job of clearing lanes through beach obstacles. The engineers would also have to blow up concrete fortifications.

A wide variety of special vehicles had been developed for the landing. The Americans developed the DUKW. This was a two-and-a-half-ton truck encased in a steel boat hull. It was equipped with both wheels and boat propellers so that it could be launched from a ship at sea, travel to the beach, then become a land vehicle once on shore.

There was also the DD (Dual Drive) amphibious tank. These would be the first heavy weapons to reach shore. The DD was a swimming tank, kept afloat by canvas balloon skirts and fitted with screw propellers powered by the tank's engines. It was a miracle that designers could come up with such a device to float the 33-ton Sherman tank. It would be another miracle if they survived the gunfire and underwater obstacles of Normandy.

The English came up with several modifications of the Sherman and the Churchill tank for surmounting obstacles, minefields and for wiping out fortified German strongpoints.

There was the Crab or Flail tank. This was a minesweeping tank. Fitted to the front of it was a long steel extension which supported a whirling drum. Attached to the spinning drum were lengths of chain which beat the ground in front of the tank, harmlessly exploding mines in the tank's path.

The AVRE (Armored Vehicle Royal Engineers) was specially designed to knock out German pillboxes and concrete bunkers. In place of the usual 75-millimeter gun was a short-barreled spigot mortar which would fire 25-pound motar bombs at point-blank range.

One of the most frightening tanks was the Crocodile. This was a flamethrowing tank that carried an armored trailer behind it containing 400 gallons of flame fuel. The flame gun was mounted in place of a machine gun and could cover a fortified position with liquid fire from a distance of 120 yards. Even if a pillbox or bunker were sealed tightly against this weapon, the fire would still have the effect of sucking the oxygen out of these enclosed spaces, suffocating the German soldiers inside.

The British designed other tanks for putting down instant roadways so tanks and vehicles would not bog down in soft sand. One of these was the Bobbin. The Bobbin would lay down behind it a heavy canvas mat 110 yards long. Another tank, the SBG (Small Box Girder Bridge) carried a small steel bridge which could be dropped across anti-tank ditches.

In addition to these novel innovations were armored bulldozers which American engineers would use to push beach obstacles and barbed wire aside.

Three companies of the U.S. 2nd Ranger Battalion were busy preparing for an almost suicidal task. They would have to scale sheer cliffs that rose 117 feet from the Normandy beach and knock out a large gun emplacement on top. This tall rock outcropping called Pointe-du-Hoc dominated both beaches where the Americans would land. The Germans were supposed to have six 155-millimeter guns housed inside the bombproof bunker at the top of these cliffs.

But the Rangers were trained for such jobs. They equipped four DUKWs with ladders that had been borrowed from English fire engines and could be extended 100 feet up the cliff. They also fitted six landing craft with six rocket launchers each. These would fire steel anchors trailing rope ladders over the cliff.

American and British paratroopers were given a huge and difficult job. They would land by parachute and glider miles behind the beach and attempt to block any reinforcements the Germans brought to the beach. They were also to disrupt German communications and knock out heavy artillery batteries.

And the old reliable American and British infantryman would have the same sort of job he had in every war and in every battle: to attack the enemy—under fire and to overwhelm him. This time it would be against the greatest complex of coastal fortifications ever constructed and manned by a skilled and desperate enemy.

On June 4 General Eisenhower was forced to postpone the June 5 date. The worst weather in 20 years was whipping through the Channel causing six-foot-high waves. Things also looked bad for the next two days and there was a possibility the invasion would have to be postponed.

This would have been a terrible setback. The Germans would have that much more time to lay mines and reinforce their positions. The extra days or weeks also might give the Nazis time to find out exactly where the invasion was aimed. It would be a wonder if they had not already guessed.

On the morning of June 5 General Eisenhower, General Montgomery, who would lead the Allied ground forces, and the rest of the Overlord admirals, air marshals and generals met at Allied headquarters near Portsmouth, England.

To the surprise of almost everyone present, the chief meteorologist for Ike's headquarters, British RAF Captain J.N. Stagg, informed the group that the bad weather over the Channel and Normandy would clear the next morning for about 36 hours. This was the break the Allies needed.

Now it was up to Eisenhower. Even though the weather would be better for a little more than a day, it would worsen again after that. If it got bad enough, it could prevent ships from resupplying the beachhead. It could keep Allied bombers from making their runs. It would be very risky.

Ike knew that the lives of hundreds of thousands of men and the fate of the whole world rested on the next decision he would make. General Montgomery said, "I would say go." But some of the other commanders pointed out the risks.

Finally Ike said, "I don't like it but there it is. I don't see how we can do anything else. Okay. We'll go!"

Gen. Dwight D. Eisenhower gives the order of the day, "Full victory—nothing else," to paratroopers somewhere in England, just before they boarded airplanes for the invasion of Normandy June 6, 1944.

CHAPTER IX: *Airborne*

In the first few minutes of June 6, D-Day, hundreds of C-47 cargo planes were warming up and taking off from air bases in southern England. Into the night sky they carried the first groups of 23,000 British and American troops of the U.S. 101st and 82nd and the British 6th Airborne divisions.

Some of the C-47's carried paratroopers loaded with weapons and ammunition. Others towed engineless aircraft on long nylon ropes. These gliders, made of wood and canvas, were designed to be pulled through the sky until they were over their destination. Then the glider pilot would cut the 300-yard-long connecting cord and steer his silent machine down through the moonlight, landing it in an open field. The gliders carried as many as 30 troops or an equal weight of vehicles or equipment.

Landing ahead of the gliders and paratroopers were the Pathfinders. These specially-trained soldiers would parachute ahead of the main landings to mark drop zones in open fields using signal lights and radio beacons.

The job of the British 6th Airborne was to capture and hold several bridges crossing the Orne River and Caen Canal and to demolish five other bridges spanning the Dives River. They were also assigned to dig in and hold the countryside from the town of

Caen to the beaches. Some of the glider troops were given the task of destroying a heavily defended gun battery which could be used against the British invasion beaches.

Most of the 6th's gliders made safe landings near Caen. The Germans in this area had planted anti-glider poles in the fields but had not yet attached mines to them. One British glider landed with its nose in the barbed wire surrounding one of the target bridges.

The twin bridges over the Orne and the Caen Canal were taken by British airborne troops after a 15-minute shootout which dazed and overwhelmed the German garrisons guarding them. Men on both sides were killed and wounded. Now the same group of Englishmen would have to hold the bridges until they were joined by the main body of troops landing later in the day on the beaches.

In the meantime, other British paratroopers were being dropped in the wrong areas or scattered by the winds. The same was happening to some of the American airborne units.

In order to round up troops in the darkness, the British used hunting horns whose mournful notes sounded across the wide Normandy fields where English paratroopers were landing.

While the twin bridges were being captured, other British airborne soldiers were fighting their way toward the bridges over the Dives. These were captured through the night and blown up by airborne who had brought vehicles and high explosive along in the gliders.

Probably the bloodiest early contact between British and German troops was at Merville near the point where the Orne River runs into the Channel. Here the Germans had a battery containing four huge naval guns which could sweep the British landing beaches with deadly fire. The position was protected by several feet of steel and concrete making it virtually bombproof. It was surrounded by thick layers of barbed wire, mine fields, mortar and machinegun positions and even an electrified fence. Two hundred Germans manned these defenses.

The British Ninth Airborne Battalion had the job of capturing these guns. Of 750 men in the battalion, only 160 were dropped close enough to the battery to attack it. To make matters worse, most of the weapons and equipment needed to assault such concentrated defenses were also scattered to the winds. Two 20-man gliders were supposed to land on the roof of the battery. They circled the massive battery for several minutes waiting for a motar flare signal telling them to land. The mortar had been lost, however, and the gliders finally veered off and landed elsewhere.

With the weapons they carried on their backs, rifles, one heavy machine gun, grenades and a few Bangalore torpedos (pipe-like lengths of explosive for blowing barbed wire), the 160 Englishmen attacked the battery. Many of the airborne soldiers were killed by mines as they cut through the barbed wire and hurled grenades into pillboxes. One lay in a pool of his own blood, screaming to his comrades to stay away from him because he was surrounded by mines.

Eighty paratroopers were killed or severely wounded but as the final shots were fired the British had captured the battery. Of the 200 German defenders 178 died in the quick, bloody battle.

The Cotentin Peninsula is a thumb-like body of land about 20 miles long and 10 miles wide jutting out into the Channel from Normandy. The westernmost landing beach, Utah Beach, where the American 4th Division would come ashore, lay at the eastern base of the peninsula.

Three German divisions were spread out across the peninsula and one was based just south of the peninsula. The low-lying areas just behind Utah Beach had been flooded by the Germans to the extent that the beach was an island connected to the rest of Normandy by five causeway roads.

It would be the job of the two American airborne divisions, 101st and 82nd, to seize and hold the base of the peninsula, blocking the movement of German troops to Utah Beach. The paratroopers would also capture the five causeways leading from the beach as well as a system of locks near the town of Carentan which controlled the flooding of the fields behind Utah.

Other objectives for the U.S. airborne force were the capture of a six-gun coastal battery at St. Martin-de-Varreville behind Utah Beach, the strategic crossroads town of Ste.-Mere-Eglis, and several bridges over the Merderet and Douve Rivers and the Carentan Canal.

Like the British, the Americans also had to clear fields for glider reinforcements that would be landing later in the day.

The Americans were scattered as badly or worse than the British. Men landed in rivers, gardens on the roofs of houses, in the midst of frightened cattle, and in the backyards of Norman farmers. Many came down in the fields flooded by Rommel's engineers and drowned before they could cut away their heavy equipment.

At Ste.-Mere-Eglise, which lay almost in the center of the American drop zones, the German garrison killed dozens of 82nd troopers as they dropped into the town. Later, other 82nd soldiers would capture the town and kill most of the Germans.

Since the landings were so scattered the Germans were confused by reports coming in all over Normandy of parachute landings. To further confuse them, Allied planes parachuted straw dummies and dropped fireworks—to simulate gunfire. Many German commanders believed the Normandy landings were a diversion to draw attention from a main thrust at Calais. Others thought it may just be a commando raid to keep the Germans awake.

All through the night Allies and Germans tangled in brief firefights and killed and captured each other. As badly as the landings had been scattered, the Americans slowly regrouped and began to capture towns and bridges. Some units lost all or most of their heavy weapons but paratroopers were trained to fight with very little.

As morning approached more than 3,000 Allied paratroopers were dead, wounded or missing. Yet most of the bridges, roads and causeways leading into the five invasion beaches had been captured.

Meanwhile, thousands of Allied bombers were dropping their deadly loads on Rommel's Death Zone. The invasion fleet, still hidden by darkness, was on the horizon.

Glider borne troops crossing the Channel above ship of the Royal Navy. In the background are the battleships Warspite and Ramillies.

Rifles ready, American paratroopers who landed inland from French Normandy coast beachheads search out a cemetery in an unidentified French town, seeking to flush out any German snipers who might be in hiding among grave stones.

Here is a cross section of the massive glider operations during the Normandy Invasion, at an objective of the U.S. 9th Air Force. Gliders and tow planes are circling and many gliders have landed in fields at left and in middle distance. Note smashed glider at lower right.

Gliders loaded with U.S. paratroops and towed by C-47's of the Ninth Air Force troop carrying command head in over the coast of France for the invasion of the Continent, leaving the English Channel behind.

CHAPTER X: *Confusion*

As Allied paratroopers and gliders were dropping from the skies over Normandy, Field Marshall Rommel was not even in France. He was at home in Germany, asleep. He had left a few days earlier to be with his wife on her birthday, June 6. He also planned to visit Hitler to plead again for more troops.

Rommel's absence illustrates how little the Germans knew about the time and place of the invasion. Basing their theory on previous Allied amphibious operations in North Africa, Sicily and Italy, the Germans believed the landings would come at high tide. The Allies had followed this habit because troops had less open beach to cross under fire at high tide. Rommel figured the next good tides would not come until June 20.

German meterologists had informed Rommel's staff that an invasion was impossible at least through June 8. The weather was too bad. The Germans lacked the weather stations in Iceland and Greenland that the Allies had.

German radar stations along the French coast had been temporarily knocked out by heavy Allied bombing but many had been put back into working order just before D-Day. And there were some sound detection facilities along the Channel for picking up the distant noises of ships or aircraft coming toward the coast.

To confuse these electronic listening posts Allied planes dropped balloons along the Dieppe-Calais coast. Attached to these balloons were metal reflectors which German radar would interpret as squadrons of aircraft. Other planes dropped thousands of pieces of metal foil which further confused the radar operators.

At the same time, high-speed Allied boats were moving down the same coast. These launches were equipped with loudspeakers which amplified recordings of ship and landing craft noises. This would be interpreted by the Germans as an invasion fleet moving toward Calais.

These tricks, as well as all the false rumors and phony radio traffic of operation Fortitude, would continue to befuddle the Germans for weeks after D-Day.

The exact time and place of the invasion had been broadcast over the BBC (British Broadcasting Corporation) and had been heard by the Germans. The BBC daily broadcast to Nazi-occupied countries musical programs and dramas as well as propaganda and news.

Inserted into these programs were often coded messages for anti-Nazi resistance fighters in the occupied countries. Certain cells of the French resistance had been given tasks to be carried out just before D-Day. These included blowing up bridges, planting mines in roads, cutting telephone lines and disrupting railroads.

The code for the guerrillas in Normandy was two lines of a well-known poem. When the first line of the poem was broadcast it would mean the invasion would come in two weeks. When the second line was heard on the radio it would mean the invasion was just 48 hours away.

German counterespionage agents had infiltrated

many cells of the French underground and had learned the various pre-invasion codes. On June 1, German intelligence personnel heard the first half of the code phrase for the Norman underground and on June 5, they heard the second half of the poem—signalling the invasion would come within two days.

This was reported to Rundstedt's and Rommel's headquarters, but for the most part these reports were ignored. The weather in the Channel seemed far too nasty for an invasion. Not a single German patrol boat had been sent out June 5, nor did the Luftwaffe try to put any reconnaisance flights into the stormy skies.

But despite these handicaps, and despite an almost non-existent navy and air force in France, the Germans would hold a numerical advantage in troops over the Allies—an advantage that could stop the invasion.

When Allied landing craft hit the five invasion beaches at 6:30 a.m. on June 6, the British and American troops would immediately face three German infantry divisions dug solidly into the Atlantic Wall. Four more Wehrmacht divisions were within 30 miles of the beaches as well as two panzer divisions. Within 100 miles of the assault area were seven more infantry and four more panzer divisions.

After the first day's landings the Allies expected to have six divisions on the beaches as well as the three airborne divisions inland—a total of nine. If the Germans reacted fast enough they could overwhelm the British and American invaders with sheer numbers. In France alone there were 50 German divisions.

CHAPTER XI: *H-hour*

The Channel was still cloaked in darkness as the Allied invasion fleet neared the coast of France and began deploying itself for the greatest military offensive in history. The weather was still nasty. High ocean swells and 20 m.p.h. winds had already swamped and sunk a few of the smaller craft. Many of the troops were too seasick to worry yet about the coming battle.

Protecting the 4,000 landing ships and craft that carried six fully-equipped army divisions were hundreds of warships and armed patrol craft on the flanks. Overhead roared thousands of aircraft through the dark sky—some of the 11,500 Allied planes assigned to Overlord.

Despite the determined efforts of the minesweepers, some ships and boats would be sunk by mines in the Channel. Rommel had seeded the coastal waters with magnetic mines that exploded when a mass of steel such as a ship passed nearby. There were also acoustic mines, detonated by the sound of a ship's propellers, and free-floating mines which blew up when struck by a vessel's bow.

The first ship to be sunk was the minesweeper U.S.S. Osprey which struck a mine. All but six of her sailors were fished from the Channel by rescue craft.

Sixty convoys of ships—LST's, warships, troopcarying ocean liners, landing craft and barges, patrol craft, tankers and merchant vessels—had split into two separate task forces off England.

The Eastern Task Force carried two British and one Canadian division headed for three beaches—Sword, Juno and Gold—stretching from the Orne River west to Port-en-Bessin. The Western Task Force carrying three American infantry divisions, the 1st, 4th and 29th, converged on two assault beaches, code-named Omaha and Utah. These lay between Port-en-Bessin, west to the base of the Contentin Peninsula.

These assault areas were spread along the shores of the Bay of Seine, a 50-mile-wide crescent-shaped inlet. When the landing areas were linked together they would form a beachhead about 60 miles wide.

H-hour, the time troops were scheduled to hit the beaches, would be 6:30 a.m. for the Americans and about an hour later for the British.

As the gigantic collection of ships plowed through rough seas, Allied airborne troops were stirring up a ruckus across the Normandy night. Only one senior German officer, General Max Pemsel, second in command of 7th Army, seemed worried about the scattered paratroop landings. He put 7th Army on full alert and told Rommel's headquarters he believed this was the invasion. No one paid much attention to Pemsel, however.

At 3 a.m. German coastal radar reported the presence of a mass of ships moving south down the Channel. A Luftwaffe patrol plane flew over the area but in the darkness could only confirm there were some ships down there—the pilot could not see the enormity of the fleet. The few German naval forces in the area were alerted and three German E-boats (torpedo boats) sped out of Le Havre at 35 knots toward the unknown enemy.

More than 140 heavily-armed warships of the bombardment fleet deployed themselves into firing positions off the British and American beaches. There were battleships, cruisers, monitors, destroyers, frigates and rocket barges in numbers unprecedented in history. Some of these ships were mounted with 12 fifteen-inch guns. Each gun could hurl a 2,000-pound shell almost 20 miles.

Around 5 a.m. the faint light of dawn revealed the first hazy outlines of the French coast. To the startled Germans in their bunkers and pillboxes, the early light also revealed ships stretching from one end of the horizon to the other.

Aboard the transport ships, landing craft were being lowered into the sea and soldiers were climbing down rope nets. The larger landing ships and craft which had sailed across on their own circled the transports. Soldiers checked each other's equipment and smeared their faces with black combat camouflage. Each man carried close to 100 pounds of equipment and ammo, some even more. And on this day all carried life preservers.

At 5:30 a.m. the bombardment ships off the British beaches began firing, and they were joined 20 minutes later by the warships lying off the American assault areas. The volume of fire put out by this fleet was awesome. Every 60 seconds, 1,000 tons of steel-encased high explosive arched through the skies and crashed into the Normandy coast.

Clouds of black smoke and dust rose from the shore above the flashes of explosions.

Then from the sky, wave after wave of bombers flying almost wing to wing came over the coast and dropped thousands of bombs on top and among the German blockhouses, gun emplacements, bunkers and pillboxes. Huge gaps were torn into Rommel's belt of defenses. The whole Normandy coast was bathed in flame, smoke and shrapnel.

By now, the Germans realized some sort of invasion would take place but they wondered if this was the main thrust or a diversionary attack.

Off the Allied beaches the steel landing craft crammed with troops, tanks and an array of other weapons and vehicles assembled themselves slowly into assault formations facing the shore. Allied navy, coastguard and marine coxswains piloting the landing craft had been given detailed charts of their landing areas. These included illustrations of how the beaches looked from the Channel, painted by a famous New England seascape artist. These would do little good because the shore was concealed by thick smoke and dust.

Control launches assigned to lead the assault into the shore gave the final signal and the lines of landing craft, their diesel engines at full throttle, churned toward the beaches. The Channel was still rough and on the way into the beaches troops found themselves having to bail water out of their craft with their helmets to stay afloat. Amost 20 assault craft sank in the first wave off both beaches.

The bombing, the naval gun fire and the rockets had created great clouds of smoke on the shore. Grass fires on the bluffs behind the beaches added to the haze. As a result, the control boat leading the first wave of 4th Division troops and tanks directed them to the wrong landing area. Here there was less German opposition than elsewhere on the coast. Twenty-eight tanks who landed with the wave blasted German positions from the beach as troops poured ashore. There was some German machine gun and mortar fire and several landing craft struck mines but it was not until the third wave was beaching that the heavier 88-millimeter German guns began dropping shells among the troops and knocking out tanks.

Leading the 4th Division's assault on Utah was Brigadier General Theodore Roosevelt Jr., whose father had led another famous charge, 50 years earlier, up San Juan Hill in the Spanish-American War. Realizing the 4th Division was landing on the wrong beach, Roosevelt decided against sending the remaining boats to the correct landing area. "We're going to start the war from here," Roosevelt said.

If the 4th had landed where they were scheduled, casualties would have been higher by the hundreds. By landing on the wrong beach they encountered light resistance and fewer obstacles and mines. But on this beach there was only one exit causeway leading off the beach. At the original beach there had been two. If the Germans were able to block the single causeway, they could bottle up a whole division on the beach. Roosevelt took a chance and it paid off.

Soldiers and tanks moved off Utah and fought their way down the causeway across flooded fields behind the beach. Once across they began linking up with paratroopers of the 101st and 82nd Airborne Divisions who had been fighting on the other side of the man made swamp.

In the meantime, other 4th Division troops raced far down the beach to another exit and fought until a second causeway was cleared and the link-up was made with the paratroopers.

With two causeways now open, soldiers and vehicles moved inland. During the course of the day 22,000 men and 1,800 half-tracks, trucks and jeeps landed on Utah and moved across the causeways. On the other side of the flooded area the 4th Division troops and the paratroopers dug in and established battle lines for the expected German counterattack.

Two hundred men were lost in the Utah Beach assault. Sixty of those died in the Channel before firing a shot. On the whole, 4th Division had been lucky.

On Omaha, 10 miles to the east, things were far different.

American infantrymen, rifles ready, strike off across wide sandy beach in wake of tanks and motorized units at one assault point on French North coast during opening of invasion of coast.

Steaming in almost within rifle range of the French coast, the U.S. Navy cruiser USS Augusta looms mammoth in size in comparison to the tiny landing craft speeding toward shore.

"Ducks" (amphibious truck) and a half track follow foot troops ashore during opening of invasion of France on a 100 mile front along the Normandy coast by allied forces June 6.

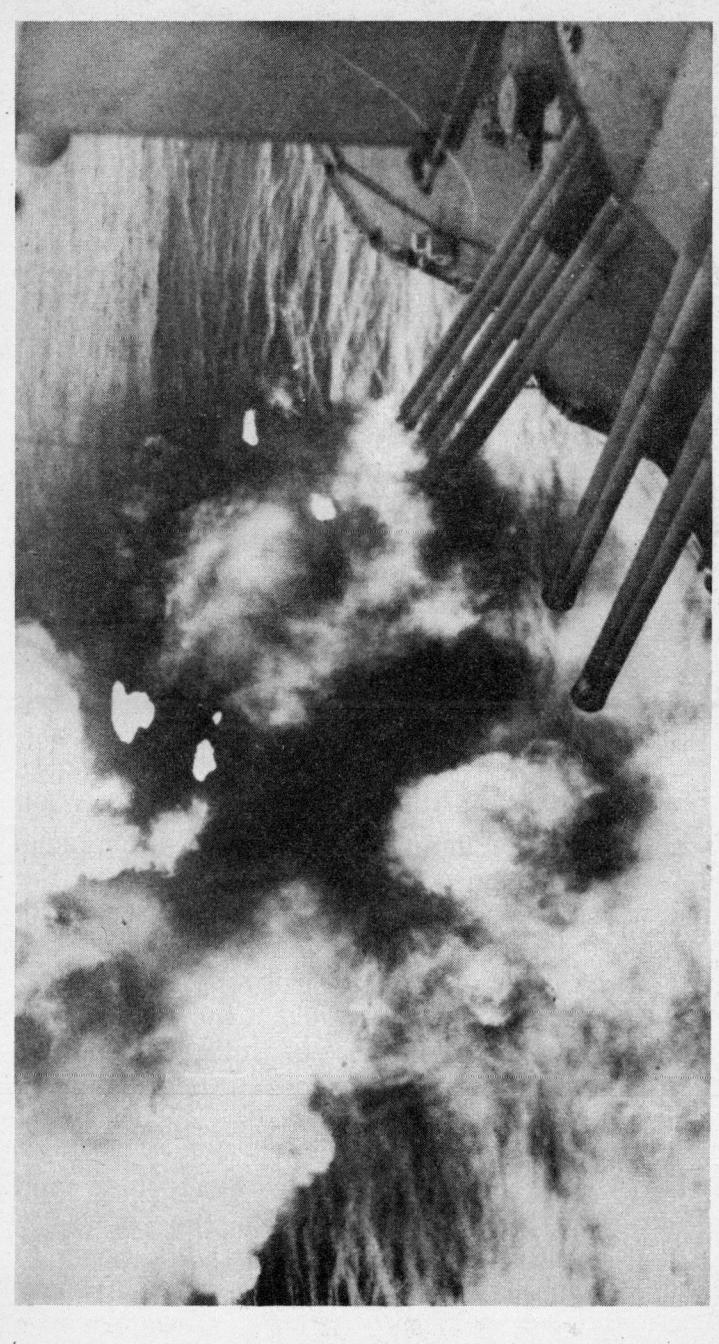

Mushrooms of smoke and flame billow out from the giant USS Nevada as the battleship provides artillery support for Allied ground forces in France by hammering enemy installations from her vantage point in the English Channel.

CHAPTER XII: *Bloody Omaha*

The battle that raged all day on Omaha Beach would go down in the history of the United States Army as one of those desperate fights whose outcome is not determined until the end of the day. Omaha Beach would rank with the battles of Bunker Hill, New Orleans, Gettysburg, Argonne Forest and Anzio. By the end of the day men would call it "Bloody Omaha".

From the beginning, the assault on Omaha Beach was a disaster. Twenty-seven of the 32 tanks assigned to land with the 1st Infantry Division were lost in a matter of minutes. After these amphibious tanks were launched from landing barges, the pounding waves ripped open the canvas balloon skirts of most of them. One after another, the 33-ton vehicles sank like stones, often drowning the crews.

The loss of these tanks would make the landing that much more costly because of the lost firepower. The rough seas had also swamped and sunk 10 landing craft of Omaha's first wave. The surviving landing craft faced other horrors.

The 29th Infantry Division was assigned to land on the western side of Omaha Beach, the 1st was to land to the east. As the landing craft got closer to shore the men could make out the deadly barrier of steel and concrete rising from the water. The obstacles were topped with mines and supported hedges of barbed wire. Beyond these were row after row of mine-capped wooden posts, exposed in the low tide. Two-hundred yards beyond the shore, across open sand, was the thin line of a seawall. And behind the seawall the ground gradually rose, ending in high bluffs and cliffs.

The objectives of both divisons would be to seize the beach exits in several areas which connected to roads leading inland. These exits were heavily guarded by German fortified positions on the cliffs.

To make matters worse, the battle-tested German 352nd Division manned the defenses along with the regular coastal defense troops. Unknown to Allied intelligence, the 352nd had taken up these positions in the spring. The American troops, expecting to meet a thin line of inferior soldiers, were instead about to face experienced and determined German defenders.

As the landing craft closed in, salvos of rockets hit the cliffs along with the combined firepower of the fleet. When the steel craft were within 400 yards of the beach, the Germans began firing. The naval and aerial bombardment apparently had left much of Rommel's defenses intact in this sector. Mortar and artillery shells threw up great plumes of white water among the boats. Other shells dropped squarely in the center of the open landing craft, exploding among the soldiers and setting the craft ablaze. Some of the craft were blown completely out of the water.

The water began to fill with wreckage and men. The dead were quiet but the living called out to their comrades in other landing craft to rescue them. Control boats quickly moved in and ordered the surviving craft to keep moving or they would cause a jam.

Some of the men in the water floated for hours before rescue boats could pick them up. Many drowned. Others died from the German machine gun fire which now stitched across the beach and clanged against the steel hulls of the craft.

The first men on shore threw themselves behind the beach obstacles for cover. Troops coming in behind them were jumping from the ramps of landing craft into three to six feet of water and wading from there to the beach. As the ramps dropped, German rifle and machine gun fire would concentrate on the craft.

Whole companies of troops were wiped out in the surf. The most intense fire came from the far ends of the beach where the two most important exits were located. As on Utah, many units were landed in the wrong place. Troops who had trained for months to knock out specific German positions found themselves on unfamiliar stretches of beach.

The Army-Navy demolition teams were being landed late and in the wrong places. Much of their equipment was lost or wrecked. Working where they were with what they had, the engineers managed to clear five paths through the obstacles instead of the assigned 16 paths. While they worked, many were shot by German snipers from the cliffs.

Despite the paths cleared through the forests of beach entanglements, men began to bunch up behind wrecked vehicles and in the water at the shoreline. Artillery and mortar rounds exploded among the masses of wet, crouching troops.

It was not long before officers and sergeants realized to stay in the water or on the beach meant death. Slowly, they crawled down the lines of waterlogged soldiers urging them to get up and run to the seawall 200 yards across the beach. One by one men began to rise and sprint for the wall. At least there was some protection there. As they reached the wall, many began to dig holes in the sand from which to fire back at the enemy.

As more and more troops reached the seawall they were able to put up an increasing volume of fire. At the same time, forward gunnery observers on the beach were giving the ships the exact positions of German emplacements by radio. Destroyers were coming in so close to the beach they were being hit by German rifle fire. The small warships began blasting bunkers and pillboxes off the beach. At the same time, the Allied air force was killing scores of Wehrmacht soldiers behind the beach.

The network of roads behind the German-held cliffs were becoming littered with the burning wrecks of German vehicles and dead and wounded soldiers. Allied fighters and bombers came out of nowhere and skimmed down roads at treetop level, raking the enemy with machine gun and automatic cannon fire.

It was not until 30 minutes after troops and tanks came ashore that Rommel was telephoned at his home in Germany. He contacted his 21st Panzer Division stationed near Caen and ordered it to the beach. It was not until 10 a.m. that the tank unit began moving down both banks of the Orne River. Rommel would take all day to get back to Normandy.

Two other panzer divisions stationed near Le Harve, a short distance from the British beaches, were told not to move unless orders came from Hitler's headquarters.

On Omaha the situation gradually improved. More engineers were coming ashore and in small teams they inched their way across the sand to German pillboxes and bunkers. While American riflemen kept the Germans pinned inside the emplacements, the engineers packed charges of TNT around the base of the bunkers and then moved back and detonated the explosives.

Other engineers crawled up to the front of the pillboxes and hurled satchels of high explosives through the gun openings. German snipers contantly picked them off from the cliffs but the engineers pushed on. By the end of the day, 50 percent of the Army-Navy demolition teams would be casualties.

Brigadier General Norman Cota of the 29th Division began organizing his men and sending them against the Germans. He walked along the seawall, oblivious of the thick rain of bullets and ordered, goaded, threatened and begged his men to get up and fight. His courage was an inspiration and all along the wall groups of soldiers began attacking the cliffs and bluffs.

Finally, in the early afternoon, using one of the three armored bulldozers that had survived from the original 16, infantrymen and engineers were able to break through the defenses. A gap was made in the center of the Omaha Beach fortifications and troops and tanks headed for the town of St. Laurent-sur-Mer.

Other Americans, once through this breach, were able to move down the high bluffs and cliffs and attack the coastal fortifications from the rear. By 1:30 that afternoon, Germans were abandoning their positions and either surrendering or fleeing. First and 29th Division soldiers captured St.-Laurent-sur-Mer and made contact with the paratroopers in that area.

A few miles west of Omaha, the 2nd Ranger Battalion suffered 50 percent casualties scaling the ten-story high cliffs of Pointe-du-Hoc. The German defenders hung over the cliffs and fired directly down on the rangers, shooting them off their ladders. Rocket-propelled ropes fired onto the cliffs were simply cut by the Germans, often after Rangers had climbed almost to the top.

The Germans also dropped hundreds of grenades on the attackers but by the end of the day, the Rangers miraculously gained the top of the cliffs and wiped out the Nazi defenders.

The six huge German naval guns the Rangers were to destroy were not on top of Pointe-du-Hoc as they had been told. The bloody day-long assault had been almost for nothing. Later a Ranger patrol found the guns in a wooded area where apparently they waited to be moved up to the cliffs. They were destroyed.

In the meantime, the British were fighting and dying to the east.

American Infantrymen wade through surf under cover of naval shell fire to make first landings on the Normandy coast of France June 6 in the opening of the Second Front. Ship from which men disembarked is at right.

American soldiers, the first to hit the French beaches, lie down in water under heavy artillery and machine gun fire from enemy pillboxes. While some of their comrades follow closely behind tanks seen plunging through the water towards the shore, those lying in the water take up position to offer what protection they can against sniping from the shore.

Troops on Omaha Beach take shelter behind seawall while awaiting orders to move inland....

American soldiers among the first to reach the French beaches, struggling through the water to the shore through a maze of beach obstacles. The water reached sometimes to the necks, and machine gunfire took its toll.

CHAPTER XIII: *Sword, Juno, Gold*

Two British and one Canadian division hit Sword, Juno and Gold beaches about an hour after the first American landings. The important crossroads towns of Bayeux on the west and Caen on the east were the main objectives. In between were the beach defenses and numerous small villages that had to be cleared of Germans.

On Sword Beach, the British 3rd Infantry Division ran into thick rows of mined barriers. Tanks of the 21st Panzer Division along the Orne River were close enough to fire shells onto Sword which was defended by several German battalions.

Half of the armored brigade that was to land with the troops was held up by bad weather and rough seas. The weather caused higher tides than expected and British engineers were unable to clear the beach. British frogmen had gone in first but had only 20 minutes to work in the rough water.

Everywhere the landing craft and amphibious tanks were sinking under the waves. Rescue boats moved about picking up the troops in the water. Other craft, however, were making it ashore, crashing through the barriers, oblivious of mines. Once through the obstacles, the commandos—used here as shock troops—and the infantrymen quickly began to move inland as German troops surrendered or died.

The 3rd Canadian Division on Juno Beach suffered identical problems as the British on Sword. But after fighting their way through the obstacles, the Canadians overran the first line of German defenses in 15 minutes of bloody hand-to-hand combat that left many dead on both sides. From there they attacked a fortified village with the help of British commandos, then raced inland for miles to make the greatest gain of any Allied forces on D-Day.

On Gold Beach, the British 50th Division fought through obstacles, mines and barbed wire while being mortared and machine gunned. Most of the fire came from the village of Le Hamel which the German 352nd Division had heavily fortified. Le Hamel lay almost in the center of Gold Beach. It took one regiment eight hours—with the loss of 200 men—to dislodge the Wehrmacht troops dug into the village. But on either side of Le Hamel the British poured ashore.

Out of the burning wreckage and mass confusion of the beaches the British and Canadians moved inland. From Sword Beach the British fought their way toward Caen. From Juno the Canadians headed toward the Bayeux-Caen highway and Caripiquet Airport 10 miles away. And from Gold the English soldiers marched toward Bayeux. Soon the men who had landed on the beaches were linking up with British paratroopers.

During the landings, the three German E-boats that had been dispatched from Le Havre somehow broke through the screen of destroyers off the British beaches. They launched 18 torpedoes at the English battleships Warspite and Ramillies but missed. Instead the underwater missiles struck a Norwegian destroyer, Svenner which was serving with the Allied fleet. The ship broke in two and sank. Thirty-four sailors died.

The E-boats successfully raced back to Le Havre, which was severely bombed over the next few days by Allied aircraft.

The 21st Panzer Division began to run into British troops along the Orne River between Caen and the coast. Artillery and rocket fire held the Germans back until darkness when they broke off the fight.

The two other Panzer divisions near the beaches did not receive orders from Hitler's headquarters until 4 p.m. They began moving but it was too late—the Allies were past the beaches and moving inland.

CHAPTER XIV: *On to Berlin!*

By late afternoon, tractors and bulldozers were clearing smoldering wreckage from the assault beaches. American and British engineers worked alongside German prisoners, clearing mines and boat entanglements from the shoreline. An occasional mortar round exploded in the sand and a few German snipers harrassed those on the beach.

Everywhere the ramps of LST's were dropping into the surf and thousands of soldiers were wading ashore. On the beaches they saw the debris of battle—discarded packs, splintered rifles, helmets, gutted tanks, bandages and bodies.

Tents with red crosses had been hastily pitched in the sand and medical teams worked to save the lives of Allies and Germans alike. Medics helped other wounded onto landing craft to be ferried out to hospital ships or to England.

Other men were busy gathering and identifying the dead who soon would be laid to rest. Cemeteries would spring up on the high ground behind the beach.

Of the 180,000 men who had landed by ship, boat, glider and parachute, 5,000 were dead and 5,000 were wounded, missing or lost at sea.

Total German casualties on D-Day were somewhere around 6,000 By the end of June,

Wehrmacht casualties would total 250,000.

Inland from the beaches, in the Norman countryside, Allied soldiers were expanding their foothold on Fortress Europe. Allied tactical bombers searched out German tank and troop formations and wreaked horror on them. Fighter planes not only blasted truck convoys and trains but chased invidual Nazi soldiers with machine gun and cannon fire.

By 9 p.m. it was safe enough to walk down most sectors of the invasion beaches without being shot.

From here the Allies would drive on toward Cherbourg and Caen, expanding the front as hundreds of thousands of fresh troops arrived from America and England.

The Germans would hold on desperately to every inch of ground but from now on they would retreat and retreat—outgunned and outnumbered.

On Allied tanks and half-tracks moving down French roads were painted slogans such as: Berlin Express! Next Stop Berlin! and On to Berlin!

In less than a year the Allies would drive the Nazi armies back into Germany and the British, American and Russian divisions would crush the remnants of the vaunted Nazi fighting machine. Hitler would kill himself.

The war would leave Germany in ruins. The Russians would occupy half of the defeated nation, the western powers would take over the other half.

Rommel, the "Desert Fox," was implicated in a plot to kill Hitler two months after D-Day. He had pleaded with Hitler to end the war after the Allies had taken half of France. Hitler's secret police forced Rommel to commit suicide.

Eisenhower, the modest victor, would go on to become President of the United States.

Britain would emerge from the war as a victorious but devastated empire. She would never regain many of her colonies and would lose others in the years to come. Today, Britain is a shadow of what she was before World War II.

The U.S. came out of the war as the mightiest nation on earth, with Russia a close second.

D-Day was but one illustration of what the free world can do when its survival is threatened. The world will probably never see another D-Day but the spirit that made D-Day a victory lives on today in America.

The countless hedgerows of Normandy were allies of the Nazis in making the advance of the British and Americans slow and bloody, after the invasion in 1944. Forty-four days of slow slugging preceded the start of the breakout July 25. Here American infantrymen go into action behind a hedge in Lessay, France. The man at left is launching a fragmentation grenade.

American assault troops in full pack reach their beachhead destination in the invasion of the Norman Coast of France on D-Day. Note massed landing craft in background, and invasion barriers erected by the Germans in the surf (upper left).

Bibliography

Adolf Hitler, John Toland, Doubleday & Company, New York, 1976.

Battle for Normandy, The, Eversley Belfield and H. Essame, DuFour Editions, Philadelphia, 1965.

D-Day—The Greatest Invasion, Editors of Army Times, G.P. Putnam's Sons, New York, 1969.

D-Day, The Normandy Invasion in Retrospect, Eisenhower Foundation, University Press of Kansas, Witchita, 1971.

European Land Battles 1944-45, Colonel Trevor Nevitt Dupuy, New York, 1962.

Fall of Fortress Europe, Fred Majadalany, Doubleday & Company, Garden City, 1968.

Longest Day, The, Cornelius Ryan, Simon and Shuster, New York, 1959.

Trail of the Fox, David Irving, Avon, New York, 1977.

Triumph and Tragedy, Winston S. Churchill, Houghton Mifflin Company, Boston, 1953.

Victory in the West—Volume I, Major L.F. Ellis, Her Majesty's Stationery Office, London, 1962.